Earth

Revised Edition

by Steven L. Kipp

Consultant:
Donald M. Scott
Aerospace Education Specialist
Oklahoma State University and
NASA Ames Research Center

Bridgestone Books
an imprint of Capstone Press
Mankato, Minnesota

Bridgestone Books are published by Capstone Press
151 Good Counsel Drive, P.O. Box 669, Mankato, Minnesota 56002
http://www.capstone-press.com

Library of Congress Cataloging-in-Publication Data
The Library of Congress has cataloged the first edition as follows:
Kipp, Steven L.
    Earth/by Steven L. Kipp.
    p. cm.—(The galaxy)
    Includes bibliographical references and index.
    Summary: Describes the surface features, interior, atmosphere, magnetic field, and
single satellite of the earth.
    ISBN 0-7368-0521-4
    1. Earth—Juvenile literature. [1. Earth.] I. Title. II. Series.
QB631.4.K57 1998
550—dc21

                                                   97-6917
                                                      CIP

Editorial Credits
Tom Adamson, editor; Timothy Halldin, cover designer and illustrator; Kimberly Danger
    and Jodi Theisen, photo researchers

Photo Credits
Bob Langevin, Night Lights Photos, Fort Smith, NT Canada,
    www.auroranet.nt.ca/nightlights, 18
International Stock/Chad Ehlers, 10; Warren Faidley, 12
NASA, cover, 1, 6 (all), 8, 14, 16, 20

1 2 3 4 5 6 05 04 03 02 01 00

Table of Contents

Relative size of the Sun and the planets

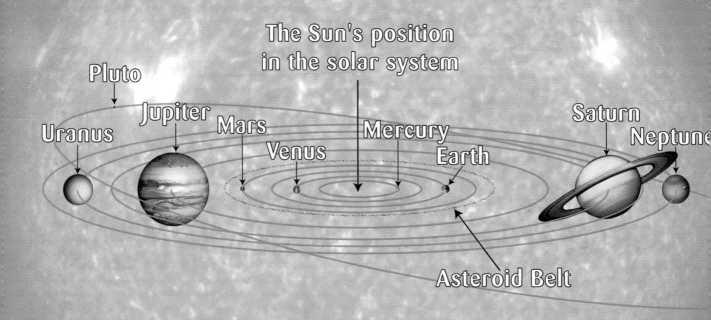

Pluto

Jupiter

Uranus

Mars

Venus

The Sun's position
in the solar system

Mercury

Earth

Saturn

Neptune

Asteroid Belt

The Sun

Earth is a planet in the solar system. The Sun is the center of the solar system. Planets, asteroids, and comets travel around the Sun.

Earth is one of the four rocky inner planets. Mercury, Venus, and Mars also are made of rock. The outer planets are Jupiter, Saturn, Uranus, and Neptune. They are much larger than the inner planets. They are made of gases. Pluto is the farthest planet from the Sun. This small planet is made of rock and ice.

People, animals, and plants live on Earth. Earth is the only place in the solar system known to have life.

◄ **This illustration compares the sizes of the planets and the Sun. Earth is the largest of the inner planets. The blue lines show the orbits of the planets. Thousands of asteroids move around the Sun. The asteroid belt is between the orbits of Mars and Jupiter.**

FAST FACTS

	Earth		
Diameter:	7,927 miles (12,756 kilometers)	**Revolution period:**	365 days, 6 hours
Average distance from the Sun:	93 million miles (150 million kilometers)	**Rotation period:**	23 hours, 56 minutes
Moons:	1		

 One moon orbits Earth. Pictures of the Moon from space show many craters and dark areas. The Moon has no clouds or oceans.

 Pictures of Earth from space show the planet's blue oceans, white clouds, and brown land areas.

People once thought Earth was the center of the solar system. They thought the Sun circled around Earth.

In the 1500s, the astronomer Nicolaus Copernicus discovered that the Sun is the center of the solar system. He found that Earth and the other planets travel around the Sun in paths called orbits. Many people did not agree with Copernicus.

Galileo Galilei was another famous astronomer. He was the first person to look at the sky through a telescope. He first looked at Jupiter in 1610. Galileo noticed that it was shaped like a ball. He also saw four moons circling Jupiter. This discovery supported Copernicus's idea that the Sun and planets do not orbit Earth. Earth and the other planets orbit the Sun. Moons orbit planets.

Space probes have taken pictures of Earth from space. The pictures show that Earth looks like a blue, brown, and white ball.

Earth sometimes is called the blue planet. Earth's oceans and atmosphere look blue from space. Water covers 70 percent of Earth's surface. Land covers the other 30 percent of Earth.

Water makes Earth different from other planets. No other planet is known to have large amounts of liquid water. Earth is the only planet known to have life. Living things need water to stay alive.

Other planets are either too hot or too cold to have liquid water. Heated water turns into a gas called water vapor. Water that is cooled can turn into ice. Mars might have liquid water below its surface. But only Earth's temperature allows all three forms of water to exist at its surface.

This symbol stands for the planet Earth. Earth is the only planet not named for a character in Greek or Roman myths. The name Earth comes from the Old English language.

Atmosphere

Earth's atmosphere lies above its surface. This mixture of gases protects Earth. The atmosphere keeps Earth from becoming too hot or too cold. The atmosphere gives living things air to breathe.

Gases make up Earth's atmosphere. The atmosphere also contains water vapor. Nitrogen makes up 78 percent of the atmosphere. Nitrogen is a gas that plants need to survive. Oxygen makes up 21 percent of the atmosphere. People and animals breathe oxygen. Other gases make up the remaining 1 percent of Earth's atmosphere.

The atmosphere also has a kind of oxygen called ozone. Ozone forms a layer high in Earth's atmosphere. This ozone layer blocks out most of the Sun's harmful rays. Pollution damages the ozone layer. People are working to protect the ozone layer. New laws help reduce pollution.

Earth's atmosphere supports life.

solid core

liquid core

mantle

crust

Earth has three layers. The core is Earth's center. It is 2,200 miles (3,540 kilometers) thick. The temperature in the core may be up to 13,000 degrees Fahrenheit (7,200 degrees Celsius). The solid core is made of mostly iron. Some of this metal has melted because of the heat. The melted metal is the liquid core.

The mantle surrounds the core. The mantle is about 1,800 miles (2,900 kilometers) thick. Heavy rocks make up this layer. Some rocks are partly melted by the heat.

The outer layer is the crust. This layer is made of lighter-weight rock. The crust is 5 to 25 miles (8 to 40 kilometers) thick. People, animals, and plants live on Earth's crust.

The crust is broken into pieces called plates. Plates slide on the melted mantle rock. These plates move very slowly. Continents are on the plates. Continents are the seven large land areas of Earth. The plate movement is called continental drift.

Liquid rock from the mantle sometimes rises to the surface through the crust. This liquid rock is called lava.

Continental Drift

All the continents once fit together. Continental drift moved them apart. The moving plates slowly change Earth's surface.

Two plates sometimes crash together. The plates push up rock to form mountains. Today, two crashing plates are making the Himalaya Mountains. Every year the mountains become slightly higher.

Cracks lie between the plates. Volcanoes form along these cracks. Lava rises through the cracks when volcanoes erupt. Lava is melted rock from the mantle layer.

The edges of two plates sometimes bump and rub against each other. This movement causes earthquakes. For example, two rubbing plates cause earthquakes in California.

The arrows show the direction that two plates slowly move to form the Himalaya Mountains.

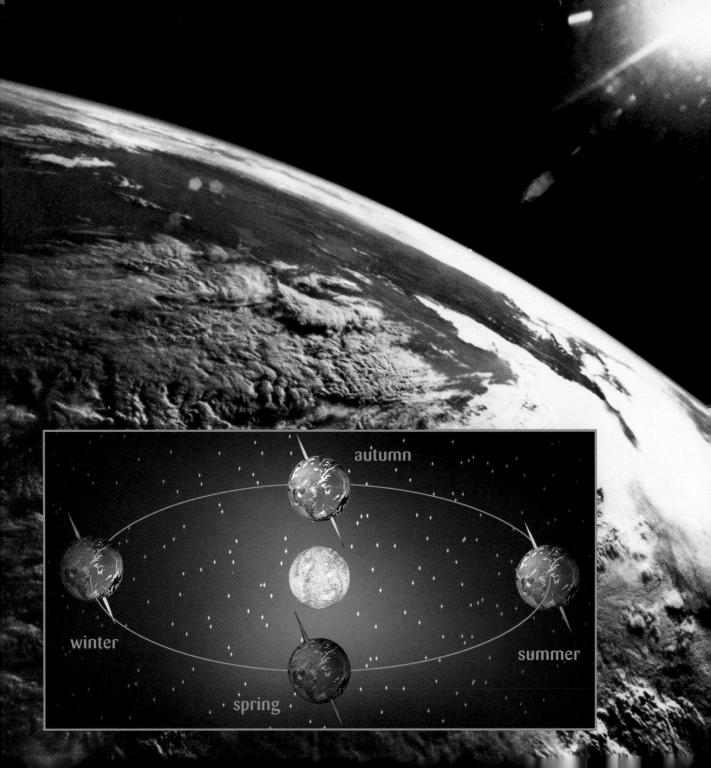

Earth moves around the Sun. One trip around the Sun is called a revolution. Earth orbits the Sun once every 365 and one-fourth days.

Earth also rotates as it orbits. The planet spins once every 23 hours and 56 minutes. Earth's rotation causes day and night. The Sun lights half of Earth at a time. While it is day on half of Earth, it is night on the other half.

Earth spins on an axis. This imaginary line runs through the north and south poles. Earth's axis is tilted. The tilted axis helps create seasons on Earth.

The north pole tilts toward the Sun in summer. The Sun's light hits the northern half of Earth more directly. The air is warmer at this time. While it is summer in Earth's northern half, it is winter in the southern half. The Sun's rays are not as direct in winter. The air is colder because the south pole tilts away from the Sun. The seasons change as Earth moves around the Sun.

The Sun lights only part of Earth at a time. The illustration shows the seasons in the northern half of Earth. Earth's tilted axis helps create the changing seasons.

Magnetic Field

Earth is like a large magnet. A magnet is a piece of metal that pulls other metal toward it.

Melted metal makes up part of Earth's core. The liquid metal flows as Earth rotates. This moving metal creates a magnetic field around the planet. The field affects other metals. It pulls some metals toward it and pushes other metals away.

Earth's magnetic field helps keep the planet safe. The field serves as a shield. It works with the ozone layer to block the Sun's harmful rays.

Earth's magnetic field sometimes traps fast moving particles from the Sun. These particles make Earth's gases glow. The glowing gases make colorful bands of light called auroras.

People can see auroras if they are far to the north or far to the south of the equator. Auroras also are called northern lights and southern lights.

Auroras appear as colorful bands of light in the sky.

The Moon

The Moon orbits Earth once every 27 days, 7 hours, and 43 minutes. The Moon is about 238,900 miles (384,400 kilometers) away from Earth. The Moon is one-fourth the size of Earth.

The Moon has many craters. Meteorites made the craters. Meteorites are pieces of space rock that sometimes crash into a planet's or a moon's surface. Comets also made some of the Moon's craters. These chunks of rock and ice orbit the Sun.

From Earth, the Moon seems to change shape. The Sun lights only part of it at one time. From Earth, only the part of the Moon that the Sun lights appears. The part that people can see is called a phase.

The Moon is the only object in space that humans have walked on and explored. On July 20, 1969, Neil Armstrong became the first person to walk on the Moon. Scientists continue to study the Moon to help them better understand Earth.

Astronauts took this picture of Earth rising above the Moon's horizon.

Hands On: The Moon's Phases

The Sun lights half of the Moon at one time. The Moon moves around Earth. Because of its orbit, the Moon seems to change shape. People see phases of the Moon.

What You Need

Basketball or soccer ball
Flashlight
A dark room
A friend

What You Do

1. Place the ball on a table. Put something next to the ball so it does not roll.
2. Turn on the flashlight.
3. Turn off the lights.
4. Have your friend shine the flashlight on the ball.
5. The ball represents the Moon. The flashlight represents the Sun.
6. Walk around the ball.

As you walk around the ball, you will notice that you can see only part of it at one time. This is like seeing the Moon's phases. The Moon's revolution around Earth causes the phases.

Words to Know

atmosphere (AT-muhss-feehr)—the mixture of gases that surrounds some planets

aurora (uh-ROR-uh)—colorful bands of light; people can see auroras in the sky if they are far north or far south of the equator.

core (KOR)—the inner part of Earth that is made of metal and melted metal

crater (KRAY-tur)—a hole in the ground made by a meteorite

crust (KRUHST)—the outer layer of Earth that is made of lighter-weight rocks

mantle (MAN-tuhl)—the layer of melted rock that surrounds the core

meteorite (MEE-tee-ur-rite)—a piece of space rock that strikes a planet or a moon

ozone (OH-zone)—a special kind of oxygen that blocks out some of the Sun's harmful rays

plate (PLAYT)—a piece of Earth's crust

Read More

Brimner, Larry Dane. *Earth.* A True Book. New York: Children's Press, 1998.

Kerrod, Robin. *Astronomy.* Young Scientist Concepts and Projects. Milwaukee: Gareth Stevens, 1998.

Vogt, Gregory L. *Earth.* Gateway Solar System. Brookfield, Conn.: Millbrook Press, 1996.

Useful Addresses

Canadian Space Agency
6767 Route de l'Aéroport
Saint-Hubert, QC J3Y 8Y9
Canada

NASA Headquarters
Washington, DC 20546-0001

The Planetary Society
65 Catalina Avenue
Pasadena, CA 91106-2301

Internet Sites

Earth Science Enterprise
http://kids.earth.nasa.gov
Let's Explore the Nine Planets
http://www.staq.qld.edu.au/k9p/title.htm
The Space Place
http://spaceplace.jpl.nasa.gov/spacepl.htm

Index